Original title:
The Glow of Christmas Wonder

Copyright © 2024 Creative Arts Management OÜ
All rights reserved.

Author: Milo Harrington
ISBN HARDBACK: 978-9916-94-046-4
ISBN PAPERBACK: 978-9916-94-047-1

A Brush of Gold on the Silent Night

In a forest dressed in white,
Elves are dancing, what a sight!
Reindeer prance with joyful flair,
While snowmen share their holiday hair.

Santa's belly shakes like jelly,
With cookies stacked, oh what a deli!
His sleigh is stuck in a tree so tall,
He waves to the kids and starts to fall.

Wishes Kindled in the Ember's Glow

Mittens hang where stockings go,
Cats dive in with sneaky flow.
Pies are cooling on the sill,
While doggies wait with eyes to thrill.

The fire crackles, popcorn flies,
And Auntie Mary attempts to bake pies.
With every laugh, the temps will rise,
We toast marshmallows under the skies!

Snow-Dusted Dreams and Laughter's Echo

Kids are rolling balls of snow,
For only one can make a foe.
Snowball fights and squeals of glee,
As snowflakes land on grandma's tea.

A penguin slides down a hill,
Spinning 'round, it gets a thrill.
Who knew winter could be so vast?
With tricks and treats, the fun's a blast!

Wonders Hidden Beneath the Stars

Stars above twinkle with glee,
Where's that star? It's lost, you see!
With a telescope, we shout and cheer,
But Grandpa's hat is now quite near.

Under the tree, gifts are piled high,
One rolls away, oh my, oh my!
Taking bets on who will chase,
Laughter echoes in every place.

Magical Threads Woven in Starry Skies

Under twinkling lights, the elves do prance,
They slip on ice, and take a chance.
With cocoa spills and giggles galore,
Who knew that reindeer could dance on the floor?

The presents are bouncing, a jolly old sight,
One rolls away, oh what a fright!
Tinsel is tangled, the cat's in a tree,
A holiday circus, come laugh with me!

A Symphony of Brightness and Wonder

Each ornament's face tells a tale so absurd,
Like grandpa who sneezed, it flew like a bird.
The chicken on the tree seems a bit out of place,
Maybe it flew here with style and grace!

The cookies are baking, but so is the dog,
He snatched a plate, put on quite the smog.
Our jolly little chef now hides under a chair,
With crumbs in the air and flour in hair!

Secrets of the Night in Festive Dreamscapes

Candles are flickering with a flick of a hand,
Dad thought he'd help, now we're lost in the sand!
The tree's now a beach, with shells and a star,
I guess festive spirit travels near and far!

The night is quite chilly, oh what a delight,
But Auntie's in shorts, she's ready to bite.
With hot cocoa spills and marshmallows on the floor,
We'll all joke about it forevermore!

Flickering Flames of Hope and Joy

The fire is crackling, with a pop and a snap,
Dad's old sock puppet has fallen in a gap.
With giggles and snorts, he dances on high,
While we roast our marshmallows under the sky!

Nearby, the snowman is sporting a hat,
But it's really a bowl that he placed on a mat.
The carrot's still grinning; he knows he's a star,
He might even make it to Santa's last bazaar!

Illuminated Paths of Kindness

In the market, folks shop fast,
Grannies zoom in freely, what a blast!
With a cart full of treats and a taco hat,
They steal our hearts—imagine that!

Twinkling lights on every door,
One cat climbs high, it's quite the score!
Knocking over boxes, it's pure delight,
With laughter ringing through the night!

Stars Adorned in Festive Grace

Oh, look at the reindeer in their suits,
Dancing like they're in funky boots!
One is stuck in a garland spree,
We all laugh so hard, can't help but see.

The snowman slips while holding his drink,
Wait, is that a hat or a stuffed pink sink?
He wobbles and jiggles, it's quite the sight,
In this winter wonder, we find pure light!

The Spirit's Dance in the Quiet Night

Elves doing the cha-cha down the street,
Spilling cocoa all over their feet!
A squirrel steals brightly wrapped snacks,
As children giggle and play with their packs.

The lights all twinkle like fireflies,
Underneath the watchful starry skies,
We join the fun, we laugh and cheer,
Embracing the spirit that draws us near!

Dreams Wrapped in Ribbons of Light

Every gift holds a surprise inside,
A pair of socks that can't quite hide!
Upon the tree hangs a pickle jar,
What's next, a pet hamster? Oh, how bizarre!

With ribbons tangled in hair, it's true,
We dance it off, with a jolly crew!
Laughter echoing through the bright delight,
As dreams unwrap in the soft moonlight!

Frosty Chimes of Love's Arrival

Bells ring out with a clunky cheer,
Snowflakes dancing, just keep your beer.
Mittens lost on a snowy spree,
Hot cocoa spills, oh woe is me!

Laughter echoes through frosty air,
Candy canes hung with mischief glare.
Sledding causes a slip, a flop,
Snowman grins, says, 'Don't ever stop!'

Whispers swirl like frosty bites,
Tumbling dreams in snowy flights.
Mistletoe hangs, plans go awry,
With each kiss, we both start to cry!

Elves are tripping on candy canes,
Reindeer prancing through snowy lanes.
Laughter rings as gifts go askew,
Christmas shenanigans, a crazy brew!

Celestial Whispers on Winter's Canvas

Stars twinkle like a child's delight,
Snowflakes fall in a dizzy flight.
Carols sung with a goofy twist,
Even the cat joins in the tryst.

Comet tails in the chilly sky,
Kittens chase, oh my, oh my!
Pies in ovens, burnt to a crisp,
Spiced apple cider in every wisp.

Presents wrapped with tape on the floor,
Squeaks and squawks, there's always more!
Grandma's hat flies in the wintry breeze,
While Grandpa snorts, with a laugh, 'Just freeze!'

Ornaments fall from a tree so tall,
Bubbles bursting, the lights start to sprawl.
Gifts exchanged with a cheeky grin,
Every moment wrapped in a din!

Twinkling Lights in Winter's Embrace

Lights flicker, dance on frosty glass,
A snowman tumbles, with a funny sass.
Hot chocolate spills, nobody cares,
Marshmallows bounce like fuzzy stares.

Trees are decorated with laughter loud,
Snowball fights lead to a giggling crowd.
Pinecone owls wink from their thrones,
While the dog steals gifts, oh the groans!

Frosty breath in the winter bite,
Snowflakes swirl in an endless flight.
Santa stuck in the chimney tight,
Kids just giggle, 'What a sight!'

Frozen toes in the chilly glee,
A trip, a fall, on a slippery spree.
Holiday cheer, in every nook,
With mishaps written in every book!

Whispered Wishes on Frosty Nights

Under stars, secrets shared with delight,
Frosted windows sparkle with spite.
Gingerbread men run as we try to bite,
While laughter echoes, oh what a night!

Magic moments wrapped in a bow,
Elves go wild in the fluffy snow.
Hot dishes served, but they just slide,
As we chase each other, laughter, and pride.

Snowflakes land on a nose so cute,
Sassy snowmen shout, 'What's your loot?'
Sleds collide with a comic surprise,
As rosy cheeks begin to rise!

Wishes whispered, as we raise a cheer,
Yet another fruitcake, oh dear, oh dear!
Huddled close by the crackling fire,
Every laugh just fuels our desire!

Radiance of the Festive Hearth

The lights are up, the cookies baked,
Grandpa's snoring, and no one wakes!
The cat's in the tree, looking quite proud,
While Dad's stuck in lights, tangled like a cloud.

Mom's singing loud, off-key but bright,
While Uncle Joe's lost in a Christmas fright.
A snowman with one eye, and a carrot that's bent,
Our holiday cheer, totally unmeant!

Kids run around, their giggles abound,
While Auntie spills punch, all over the ground.
A reindeer in pajamas, just down the street,
A festive parade, we can't help but greet!

Eggnog's flowing, time for a toast,
To family and friends, that's what we love most!
With laughter and joy, let the madness unfurl,
For nothing says fun like a chaotic swirl!

Embers of Joy in the Snow

In winter's chill, we dance about,
Snowflakes fall, and so does the clout.
A snowball fight, oh what a blast,
Until someone slips, and down they fast!

With hats askew and scarves all around,
We build a snowman, the ugliest found.
His carrot's a nose, but it's a bit crooked,
No one can tell if it's happy or spooked.

Hot cocoa spills on the table bright,
As cousin Meg joins in on the fight.
Marshmallows fly like tiny white bombs,
Laughter erupts, and chaos calms.

The fire crackles, stories to share,
Wolfing down cookies, without a care.
Snowflakes dance in the dimming light,
We laugh and we play, through the chilly night!

Shimmering Dreams Beneath the Stars

Beneath the stars, the sleigh bells jingle,
But wait! The dog's stuck in a single tangle!
With stockings hung on the mantel so high,
It's a race to see who can reach for the pie.

Santa's on the roof, or so we believe,
But truth is, it's just Dad, who can't quite leave.
With reindeer ears and a belly that shakes,
He trips on the kids' toys, and oh, what breaks!

The glow of lights, all colors and sound,
While Mom holds a spatula, she'll put you in the ground!
"Who ate the cookies?" echoes through the room,
As the dog gives a grin, oh how he does bloom!

Mismatched pajamas and stories on loop,
It's a holiday chaos, the cutest of troops.
With giggles and warmth, we all take a pause,
For laughter and love are our biggest applause!

Enchanted Evenings of December

Evenings glimmer with sparkles and cheer,
The cat's on the table, oh dear, oh dear!
As Grandma attempts to dance by the fire,
We all try to keep our laughter conspired.

The kids play charades, and oh, what a sight,
Uncle Tim sings loudly, though he's not quite right.
With rumors of reindeer and stories of grace,
It's hard to keep straight with pie on your face.

Wrapping gifts wildly, a tape monster's lair,
Mom's on a mission, we're fully unaware.
A sock for a gift? What a classic old tale,
With giggles and chuckles, we dance through the hail.

Under the stars, we share treats galore,
With laughter and joy, who could ask for more?
In these merry nights, our hearts feel so light,
As we celebrate love, under the soft twilight!

Sparkling Eyes Under Starlit Canopies

Beneath the twinkling lights we gawk,
A squirrel who thinks he's Santa talks.
With wings of dreams and laughter shared,
The magic's real, and we all dared.

We hang our hopes on every branch,
While giggles float in every glance.
The chilly air, it bites our nose,
But joy ignites from head to toes.

Our hats are crooked, scarves askew,
As snowmen plot to join our crew.
They dance with glee, then slip and slide,
A winter race, we can't abide.

We cheer the snowball fights we win,
Then trip and fall, we laugh again.
With frosty wonders all around,
The spirit's felt, no need for sound.

Frosted Wishes and Warmth of Home

A cookie thief with sneaky paws,
Claims all the treats without due cause.
Mom warns him not to take the pie,
But he just grins, oh my, oh my!

The cocoa spills, the marshmallows fly,
As dad's attempts to cook go awry.
With every splash, we burst in mirth,
An epic tale of kitchen worth.

The glow of lights through frosty panes,
Each bulb reveals our silly gains.
We twirl 'round trees, we laugh and cheer,
Creatures of glee, we meddle near.

The chill outside becomes our cloak,
As giggling curls from cheeks unbroke.
In every crack with laughter found,
A merry scene, a joyful sound.

A Tapestry of Colors in Winter's Hand

A rainbow scarf, mismatched it seems,
Worn by a kid with big, bold dreams.
As snowflakes fall, they flutter in,
His style's a win, oh where to begin?

We build snow forts, the wall is grand,
With lofty hopes, we take a stand.
Then with a flop, we fall inside,
The snowy fortress, how we glide!

A fashion show of boots and hats,
Where everyone's a winner—chats.
With mittens lost and pants now damp,
We strike the pose and make our stamp.

The colors swirl beneath the sky,
Where every snowman waves good-bye.
Hand in hand, we laugh aloud,
Facing the winter, so proud we're proud.

The Embrace of Light on Darkest Nights

When darkness falls, the laughter stirs,
We dress like elves, all giggles and furs.
With every light that twinkles bright,
We frolic, free, into the night.

Our shadows dance on walls of frost,
We find the fun in what is lost.
The stars above watch us take flight,
A merry crew, so full of light.

The chaos blooms, a silly sight,
As we trip over gifts, it feels so right.
With every cheer, the winter glows,
As laughter flows, the magic shows.

So raise a toast with cups of cheer,
The craziness brings everyone near.
For in this joy, our hearts unite,
Embracing warmth through frosty nights.

Twinkling Lights of Midnight Magic

Blinky lights dance on the tree,
As cats plot mischief and glee.
Ornaments swing like they're alive,
While tinsel tries hard to connive.

Snowflakes fall, they trip and slide,
Chubby squirrels run to hide.
Elves sneak snacks, a cookie feast,
Under mistletoe, they laugh at least.

Hot cocoa spills with a splash,
Marshmallows bounce in a crash.
Frosty noses tin foil shine,
The night is quirky, oh so divine!

Wrapping paper shouts and sings,
A present wriggles, oh the springs!
Laughter echoes, cheer fills the air,
Midnight magic, let's not compare.

Whispers of Frosted Dreams

Frosty fingers wave with cheer,
As snowmen dance, let's give a cheer!
In every nook, giggles take flight,
From baking cakes 'til late at night.

Reindeer snicker, prance with pride,
Wrapped up gifts, oh what a ride!
Gingerbread men with frosting crowns,
Running around in silly towns.

Chubby cheeks full of delight,
Building snow forts feels so right.
With each snowball, laughter breaks,
Even grumpy cats make mistakes!

Lights twinkle like a disco ball,
Decking the halls, we'll have a ball!
What joy to find in snowy schemes,
Chasing laughter, living dreams.

Shimmering Hearts in Winter's Embrace

Hearts aglow in winter's freeze,
With tickles of snow, we all appease.
Sledding down hills, oh what a thrill,
Clinging together, against the chill.

Elves tumble, quite a sight to see,
Wrapped in scarves, so blissfully free.
Hot cocoa in hand, marshmallows fly,
With every sip, a goofy sigh.

Carolers sing the most offbeat tunes,
While pine-scented air makes us swoon.
Mittens found in a snowy pile,
Have hearts warming with every smile.

Under the stars, cookies galore,
Stumbling home like never before!
With joy as our guide, we dance and cheer,
Shimmering hearts, winter draws near.

Stardust on Evergreen Boughs

Evergreen trees, a jolly sight,
Adorned with stardust, shining bright.
Birds giggle, swing from the bows,
Chirping tales of holiday vows.

Tinsel rains from a minor fall,
Kittens pounce with a fuzzy sprawl.
Garland tangled in a funny way,
What a ruckus, we dance and sway!

Pinecone goblins with silly hats,
Crack open nuts, oh the chitchats!
Sipping cider, we toast with cheer,
Under starlights, all draw near.

As night falls, the fun begins,
With every laugh, let's pile in!
Stardust glimmers, a colorful sight,
Creating memories, pure delight.

A Symphony of Crystalline Light

In the town where snowmen prance,
The carrot noses do a happy dance.
With scarves so bright, they twist and twirl,
As winter winds give them a whirl.

Tinsel tangled on the tree,
The cat's the one in disarray, you see.
Wrapping paper, torn in glee,
A gift for me, oh look at he!

Cookies baked with sprinkles bright,
The dog is aiming for a bite.
Fondant figures, oh so sweet,
But now they're looking like a treat in defeat!

So raise your glass of bubbly cheer,
To silly socks and holiday beer!
With gleeful jigs and silly sights,
We celebrate these cozy nights.

Flickers of Hope on Winter's Breath

On frosty nights, the lights ignite,
A squirrel skids past, a comical sight.
With little hats upon their heads,
They scurry about, ignoring their beds.

Snowflakes fall like popcorn bursts,
While mittens disappear, oh what a curse!
The kids build forts with snow and glee,
While parents pray for sanity!

Eggnog spills on the cheerful rug,
The dog takes credit with a shrug.
As hiccups and laughter fill the air,
Someone's got glitter in their hair!

So gather round the roast so bright,
The turkey's singing with all its might.
With tickles and jokes, we'll have a show,
Together we thrive in the winter glow.

Glimmers of Love in Every Shadow

Underneath the starry night,
The cookie jar's gone, what a fright!
With crumbs scattered, a sugary trace,
Clever kids with a sneaky face.

Lights blink on the neighbor's tree,
While raccoons wrestle in harmony.
They feast on leftovers from the night,
And the holiday spirit shines so bright!

Stockings hung with candy corn,
But now they're empty, all is torn.
A game of hide and seek begins,
As family bickers over silly wins.

Now the fireplace crackles with cheer,
As laughter echoes far and near.
With mugs of cocoa, smiles are wide,
In this season where joy's our guide.

Echoes of Laughter in the Chill

The carolers sing, but croak a note,
While ducks in hats try to stay afloat.
Chickens dance along the street,
Creating a rhythm that's hard to beat.

Snowball fights turn into slip and slides,
With laughter erupting, no one hides.
As mittens fly and tempers flare,
It's all in fun, we hardly care!

Grandma's slippers, fluffy and neat,
Become the highlight of the festive greet.
"Who wanted this?" she shouts with glee,
While wearing tinsel bling, look at me!

So let us cheer, raise your cup high,
The jokes, the giggles never die.
In chilly air, with hearts so warm,
We'll dance through winter's quirky charm!

Faeries of Light on the Icy Air

In the chilly air, faeries prance,
Wearing socks that make them dance.
They twirl around with glee so bright,
Painting snowflakes with pure delight.

Tiny wings that flutter and spin,
Stealing cookies, oh what a sin!
They giggle as they sweep the ground,
Leaving candy trails all around.

With snowmen grinning from ear to ear,
These mischievous faeries bring us cheer.
They'll drop a snowball, take cover fast,
Laughing loudly, their fun unsurpassed.

So if you see a twinkle or two,
It's giggling faeries just for you.
With joyful noise they fill the night,
In their frosty realm of pure delight.

Chasing Fireflies Through Snowy Nights

In winter's chill, fireflies roam,
Dressed in sweaters, far from home.
They wink and blink in frosty air,
Chasing shadows without a care.

With each soft glow, they take a chance,
To dart away in a silly dance.
Snowflakes tumble, a shimmer they find,
But those fireflies leave the cold behind.

Laughter echoes as they play,
But oops! One tripped on a frozen sleigh.
With giggles bright, they rise once more,
As snowballs fly, they start to roar!

A comical sight, they float and sway,
Bright flashes of cheer on a snowy way.
Let laughter ring through the frosty night,
As fireflies paint the world in delight.

Celestial Wonders Above the Pines

Up above the pines so tall,
Stars are playing a game of ball.
They bounce around, giggle and shine,
Drawing wishes with every line.

Shooting stars with silly hats,
Dodging planets like playful cats.
The moon beams down, a jolly friend,
As spacey jokes they wisely send.

Galaxies spin in dazzling style,
While comets pause to wink and smile.
And if you catch them in the night,
They'll tickle you with pure delight.

So gaze above, let laughter soar,
With celestial wonders, who could want more?
In this cosmic dance, let's all partake,
As the universe giggles, we shake!

Glorious Hues of the Winter Sky

The winter sky wears colors bold,
Peachy pinks and icy gold.
Birds in coats of fluffy white,
Laughing as they take their flight.

Each sunset, like a painted show,
Where wacky clouds all seem to glow.
With cotton candy drifting high,
The sky is laughing, oh my, oh my!

As night falls down, light twinkles bright,
Stars descend to join the night.
They play a game of hide and seek,
While winter's air gives a chilly tweak.

So come outside, let laughter rise,
Under glorious hues, 'neath winter skies.
With a sprinkle of joy, we'll dance about,
As the night unfolds, there's no doubt!

Candles Flickering in Silent Prayer

In the corner, candles sway,
Creating shadows that dance and play.
The cat leaps up, swats one low,
Knocking over gifts all aglow.

A nutcracker grins, a sight so silly,
Beneath the tree, it seems so frilly.
Grandma giggles, spills her tea,
As the lights twinkle, wild and free.

Funny socks wrapped with care,
Uncle Bob wears one, a quirky pair.
The lights will blink, the kids are wild,
To be merry, it's all reconciled.

Whispers shared 'neath the festive dome,
With laughter echoing—this is home.
Candles flicker, no time to fret,
With joy all around, we won't forget.

Magic Beneath the Mistletoe

In the kitchen, chaos reigns,
With flour flying, baking pains.
Grandpa sneaks a cookie bite,
Under mistletoe, it's love at sight.

A puppy barks, chasing around,
Tangled in ribbons, he's newly crowned.
Dancing pairs beneath the leafy spray,
One slips—oy vey! Hooray, hooray!

Chocolates wrapped, a prank in store,
Uncle Fred finds a soft sticky floor.
Laughter erupts, bright as a star,
Kissing under mistletoe—a real bizarre.

With every giggle, the day's delight,
A family gathering, all feels right.
Amid our antics, we all agree,
Magic is here, oh joy, oh glee!

Illuminated Moments in the Dark

Lights twinkle like fireflies bright,
While Dad searches for the switch—what a sight!
A tree that looks like it's wearing a crown,
Wobbling ornaments threaten to frown.

Sister sings off-key, a holiday song,
While the puppy joins in, barking along.
Under the glimmer, we share a wink,
In a room full of snacks, we kid, we blink.

Mom bursts out with her festive cheer,
As Dad dons a hat, slightly askew, oh dear!
Silly selfies under the radiant beams,
Where laughter erupts, bursting our seams.

In the dark, our spirits ignite,
With goofy faces, it feels just right.
Illuminated moments, let's savor these,
In our joyful chaos, we find the peace.

The Warmth of Giving Hearts

Boxes wrapped with colors bright,
Tucked away, hidden from sight.
Grandma's cookies, sweet and fun,
Under the tree, we say we're done—none!

Funny hats worn with a flair,
Family portraits always an affair.
With giggles mixing in the air,
A giving heart, beyond compare.

Toys exchanged, laughter so sweet,
Finding the perfect gift is quite a feat.
In the spirit of fun, we play our part,
As the warmth of joy fills every heart.

With open arms and silly grins,
This holiday laughter, it always wins.
Amid the chaos, love takes the lead,
Feeling warm, yes, in every deed.

Hearts Illuminated by Soft Whispers

In the attic, snowmen dance,
Wearing hats and silly pants.
Elves giggle in a cluttered heap,
While reindeer play and fake-sleep.

Mittens missing, socks askew,
Hey, where's Rudolph? Who knew?!
Under ladders, twinkling lights,
Cats are chasing festive sights.

Grandma's cookies, burnt, not brown,
Who needs them? Let's wear a crown!
With fruitcake bouncing down the street,
The neighbors laugh—oh, what a feat!

But joy flows with every cheer,
As we toast with cider near.
In jolly spirits, laughter flows,
Fun times come, like fluffy snow.

Beneath the Boughs of Yuletide Grace

Beneath the tree, my dog is stuck,
With tinsel twinkling, what bad luck!
A cat climbs up for a better view,
And naps on lights that brightly ooze.

Presents wrapped in papers bright,
But where's my gift? It's out of sight!
Dad's found the eggnog, what a sip,
He's dancing now—oh, such a trip!

Songs are sung with missing keys,
As Auntie sneezes—"let's say cheese!"
We laugh till our sides begin to ache,
With every joke, the room does shake.

In this chaos, hearts unite,
With chuckles shared, pure delight.
Under boughs, we find our place,
In silly joy and warm embrace.

Frost-veiled Wishes on Gentle Winds

Wishes float on chilly air,
As puppies roll, without a care.
Snowflakes swirl in clumsy twirls,
While kids are shouting, "It's a whirl!"

Hot cocoa spills on Grandma's lap,
As laughter spreads like a sweet map.
With marshmallows high and spirits bright,
We stack them up for a frosty fight.

The tree's a tripping hazard, oh dear,
While Uncle Bob sings loud, so near.
Joyous giggles, sparkly eyes,
As siblings launch their snowball spies.

All around, the merriment grows,
With playful whispers in the rose.
Frosty wishes, warm delight,
Make this season pure and bright.

Delight in Every Glimmering Snowflake

Look at the snow, it's sparkly and round,
Oh wait, that's a snowball—what a sound!
Sledding down a hill with flair,
I flip and land in cold despair.

But laughter bubbles, we carry on,
With frosty noses, from dusk till dawn.
A gingerbread war's about to start,
With icing guns, we'll steal the heart!

Christmas sweaters, all mismatched,
Grandpa's singing? We're detached.
The tree's all shaky, full of cheer,
As cousins make their voices clear.

So let us toast with cheer all night,
Embrace the joy, in joyful plight.
In every flake, a giggle stirs,
Delight remains, as laughter whirs.

Lullabies of a Frosted Wonderland

In hats too big, we tumble down,
Chasing snowflakes, we wear a frown.
Hot cocoa spills, oh what a sight,
Mittens mismatched, still feel so right.

The reindeer laugh, they think it's grand,
When we slide down hills, unable to stand.
Snowmen wobble, with carrots for noses,
As laughter bursts, like hidden roses.

In fluffy boots, we stomp around,
Making snow angels, face to ground.
But someone sneezes, and oops! There go,
The best of snowballs, launching in tow!

So here we giggle, with cheeks aglow,
Under the moonlight, putting on a show.
The frost may bite, but we wear a grin,
In this frosted wonder, let the fun begin!

Snowflakes Dancing in Soft Glow

Snowflakes tumble, a pillow fight,
Landing on noses, oh what a sight!
We chase them down, but oh, so slow,
Catch one in mouth, it's cold, whoa, whoa!

Laughter weaves through each swirling flake,
Hats go flying, make no mistake.
With every slip, we giggle and squeal,
Hot chocolate spills, oh what a meal!

Frosty fingers, but spirits awake,
Winter's charm is quite the prank.
Moments arise, quite silly indeed,
As we dance 'round the tree, the snow takes heed!

So let's embrace every snowy twist,
In laughter and joy, none can resist.
With each falling flake, let merriment flow,
In this wondrous season, enjoy the show!

Heartbeats Beneath a Starry Sky

Under twinkling stars, we run wild,
Dreaming of magic, like a child.
A snowball lands, right on your nose,
Giggles erupt, like overflowing prose.

Sleds go whizzing, with faces aglow,
Who knew such speed could cause this much woe?
We crash into bushes, laughter flies high,
Making memories beneath the wide sky.

With cheeks like cherries, we sing a tune,
While the moon hangs low, a silver balloon.
The cold can't chill this joy that we share,
For our hearts beat louder, beyond all compare.

So let's chase those stars, as snowflakes fall,
In this thrilling wonder, we'll have a ball!
Every heartbeat's a story, pure delight,
In this magical moment, let's stay up all night!

Tinsel Threads of Timeless Memories

Tinsel hangs low, the kitty's on spree,
Chasing those strands, oh what a sight to see!
Mom's yelling loudly, 'Not on the tree!'
As we burst out laughing, oh so carefree.

Ornaments swinging, the cat gives a jump,
Down go the baubles, with quite a thump.
Our giggles echo, a joyful parade,
As we clean up chaos, a merry charade.

Baking cookies, we sprinkle with flair,
But flour's everywhere, like snow in the air.
With every misstep, a chuckle erupts,
In this warm kitchen, our spirits are up.

So let's gather 'round, share tales of our fun,
In this tapestry woven, oh look what we've spun!
With tinsel and laughter, and every sweet treat,
These timeless memories, make our joy complete!

Radiant Smiles in Softest Whispers

In cozy socks and clumsy glee,
The cat joins in the family tree.
With tinsel on his fuzzy head,
He swipes the gifts while we eat bread.

Laughter bubbles, joy takes flight,
As we attempt to bake just right.
The cookies burn, the laughter stays,
Tomorrow's feast is sure to amaze.

Uncle Joe dons a Santa hat,
He tells us tales, oh where's the cat?
A snowball fight, it's game on now,
Though mom will shout and furrow brow.

Hot cocoa spills and marshmallows fly,
As Grandma's dance stuns every eye.
With radiant smiles both near and far,
We'll share these tales 'neath the same star.

Dreams Wrapped in Glittering Ribbons

Prancing elves in mismatched shoes,
Sneakily hide all Grandma's snooze.
Delight and giggles fill the air,
As scents of cookies whisper, 'Stay there!'

The tree, it sparkles, looks so fine,
Wrapped in ribbons and good red wine.
Yet all the cats, they plot and scheme,
To topple dreams from a twinkling beam.

A gift appears, it's wrapped so tight,
Turns out it's socks — what pure delight!
We all burst out, a fitting jest,
For Christmas cheer brings out the best.

Dreams unfold in every gleam,
Childish laughter is the theme.
This silly joy around the floor,
Is what we cherish, and so much more.

The Dance of Light on Silent Streets

Streetlights shimmer, twinkle bright,
As neighbors bicker, 'Did you bite?'
The lawn decorations sway in time,
A snowman whispers, 'Where's my lime?'

Down the lane, the laughter grows,
While Santa's sleigh has lost its nose.
The festive hats atop our heads,
Are filled with dreams, like warm beds.

Frosty mugs and gingerbread,
Silly antics, nothing said.
While sleds go flying down the hill,
We tumble down, and what a thrill!

Underneath the moonlit skies,
Glowing faces and joyful sighs.
The funky dance of winter's cheer,
Will stay with us throughout the year.

Illuminated Pathways of Shared Laughter

Footprints in snow tell tales galore,
As grandma's baking stirs up lore.
With giggles echoing through the night,
We share our stories in pure delight.

Spotted reindeer on the roof,
Uncle's jokes are quite the goof.
Each bright bulb flickers, lights the scene,
As we toast to wishes, just like a dream.

A jingle bell or clattering spoon,
Echoes soft like a distant tune.
With frosty cheeks and silly grins,
We gather close, where the fun begins.

Shared laughter lights each winding street,
With every moment, our hearts compete.
In this merry, wonky dance,
We find the joy, take our chance.

Heartfelt Embrace in the Chill

With coats too tight and mismatched hats,
We shuffle about, like clueless brats.
The snowflakes fall, they bite and swirl,
So we dance like penguins, oh what a whirl!

Hot cocoa spills down from mugs in hand,
As we try to smile, slips are well-planned.
The snowman winks, his carrot so bold,
While kids scream joy, in the frost so cold!

Uncle Joe's sweater, it's bright and loud,
He claims it's stylish, making him proud.
But when he bends, we all try to hide,
For the snowflakes laugh, they haven't died!

Gathering 'round the fireplace bright,
We roast marshmallows, oh what a sight.
But s'mores end up stuck to every face,
A feast of giggles, what a warm place!

Serenade of Stars in a Velvet Night

Under the lights, we make a scene,
Dad's karaoke, a pleasure unseen.
Singing off-key with great, hearty glee,
The cat runs away, seeking a tree!

Tinsel and sparkles, all tangled tight,
Grandma's lost her cool, what a sight!
She warbles merry, the dog joins in,
With festive howls, oh let us begin!

The cookies baked are a sight indeed,
But half are burnt, we laugh and concede.
On the floor with crumbs, we roll and play,
As sugar rush fuels the silliness sway!

Carols like cats are sung out of tune,
Under the moon, we dance till it's noon.
A holiday mix, laughter takes flight,
In the velvet night, all feels just right!

The Warmth Beneath the Frost

Outside it's freezing, the temperatures drop,
While we're in the house singing, 'No, don't stop!'
Sock puppets dance on the kitchen floor,
They wiggle and jiggle, begging for more!

Frosty the snowman, quite round and stout,
We put on his hat but then he fell out!
His carrot nose rolls – oh what a scene,
And the children giggle, forgetting their sheen!

Fireside tales with popcorn galore,
As everyone rushes to snag a score.
But Uncle Bob's joke, it's cheesy at best,
We laugh so hard, we can't get our rest!

The warmth we share, more than blankets or heat,
In laughter and love, it's a cozy treat.
So gather around and let spirits lift,
For joy is the very best, heartwarming gift!

Kindles of Joy in Every Ember

The fire crackles, a dance in the night,
But Dad spilled the logs, oh what a sight!
Embers fly, like tiny stars up high,
And Grandma yells, 'Don't let them fly by!'

Stockings are hung with great glee and cheer,
And Aunt Patty's snoring is all that we hear.
With cookies gone missing, we raise a toast,
To finding them quick as we giggle and boast!

A snowball fight got wildly absurd,
When old man Jenkins was lovingly stirred.
He slipped and he fell, let out a yelp,
We laughed till we cried, all by ourselves!

With fun and frolic filling the days,
The spirit of joy forever stays.
In every ember, love's flickering light,
Brings warmth to our hearts, on this merry night!

A Treetop Dance of Joyful Wishes

Up on the tree, the ornaments swing,
The pets stare up, what a sight to bring.
A cat in a hat, a dog with a bow,
They both want the star, oh, what a show!

Fairy lights twinkle, like fireflies in cheer,
A message from Santa, or could it be beer?
Cookies gone missing, crumbs on the floor,
Who's nibbling treats? I'd like to know more!

Snowflakes come tumbling, a comic ballet,
The kids make a snowman who's ready to play.
But the snowman falls down, takes a dive with a laugh,
Now he's stuck in the gutter, what a silly gaffe!

So here's to the season, with giggles and glee,
May your holidays sparkle, like every good spree.
With laughter and joy, let's unwrap the delight,
Share silly moments all through the night!

Hearts Aglow in Solstice Light

Lights all around, the house looks so bright,
Dad tripped on a cord, oh what a fright!
The dog grabbed the tinsel, now he's a tree,
We'll call him our mascot, our dear jubilee.

Hot cocoa spills over, a marshmallow flood,
The kids are all bouncing, stuck in the mud.
Grandma jokes lightly, with a wink and a grin,
Her holiday sweater's a total win-win!

Mittens and scarves, oh, what a strange sight,
A squirrel steals a cupcake, oh what a delight!
Everyone's laughing, 'cause who could resist,
The charms of this season, wrapped up in a twist?

So gather the fam, let's spread all the cheer,
With jokes and warm hugs, let's toast with a beer.
In this merry moment, we'll shine as we may,
With hearts all aglow, let the fun lead the way!

Crystalline Dreams Underneath the Moon

Under the moonlight, the snowflakes do twirl,
A penguin in spectacles dances, oh swirl!
The kids built a snow fort, think they're all kings,
But snowballs come flying, igniting their flings.

A rabbit with earmuffs hops into the fray,
He steals all the carrots, the kids shout, hooray!
They chase him through drifts, in this wintery spree,
Who knew that the snow could be so wild and free?

Gentle frost gathers on noses and cheeks,
But laughter erupts as the banter peaks.
A snowman with sunglasses guards all the fun,
He's the coolest of all in this winter sun.

So let's raise a glass to the icy delight,
Full of giggles and kindness, it's truly a sight.
In crystalline dreams, let the laughter resume,
Merry moments await under bright winter's bloom!

Whimsical Whispers of Winter's Night

The night is alive with a playful parade,
A snow angel flops, a belly flop laid.
The stars twinkle brightly, a comedy scene,
As reindeer slip by, they're somewhat obscene!

Hot cider is spiced, a delight in each sip,
But someone's on skates with a rather wild grip.
They whirl and they twirl, oh what a display,
Slipping and sliding, they're life's cabaret!

Frosted branches whisper with secrets untold,
As elves do a jig, so brazen and bold.
A gingerbread house, gone missing its roof,
Now it's a race, let's find the goof troupe!

So gather your loved ones, light up the night,
With laughter and joy, everything feels right.
With whimsical whispers, let the tales unfold,
In the warmth of the season, the memories told!

Carols Amidst the Winter's Breath

Cold winds howl with joy and cheer,
Singing snowflakes dance near and dear.
A squirrel in a hat, oh what a sight,
Trying to steal the Christmas lights!

Chubby cheeks and reindeer prance,
Tripping on snowflakes, they take a chance.
The cat in a scarf, looking so proud,
Staring at the tree, a glittering crowd!

Laughter echoes from door to door,
As snowmen fall down, we laugh and roar.
The dog's dressed as Santa, what a grand view,
Chasing his tail in a red suit too!

Bells ringing out in a comical tune,
Under the glow of a silly moon.
While cookies keep vanishing into thin air,
Even the gingerbread men are in despair!

Hidden Marvels in Frosty Fields

Mittens lost in a game of tag,
Noses bright red, with a jolly brag.
The snowman wobbles, he just might fall,
With a carrot for a nose, he's having a ball!

Frosty prints lead to nowhere fun,
Chasing after friends, oh what a run!
A rabbit in boots, hopping with glee,
Looks like he's raising his own cup of tea!

Sleds tangled up in a playful fight,
"Get off!" cries a kid, "This isn't right!"
A snowball hits, the laughter takes flight,
With cheers of delight, oh what a sight!

Under the moon, we dance and glide,
Snowflakes supporting our joyful ride.
A hidden marvel, each laugh a treat,
In frosty fields, where fun and friendship meet!

Luminous Spirits on Frosty Evenings

Flickering lights on every house,
A grumpy old cat, quiet as a mouse.
Tinsel gets caught in an awkward curl,
As kids try to help with a twirl and swirl!

The dog gets dressed in a sparkly outfit,
Barking with joy, he won't quit!
Carols sung with a giggly twist,
As mom loses track, of the gifts on the list!

Lemonade stands made of icy fluff,
Selling hot cocoa, but not quite enough.
A snowglobed mishap, it's all in good fun,
Where laughter and snowflakes under the sun!

Glowing candles lighting a playful scene,
With elves in pajamas, so cozy and keen!
Their antics remind us, laughter's the key,
To shine through the chill, like a warm cup of tea!

Illuminated Memories of Yuletide Cheer

Nuts and fruitcakes on the top shelf,
A fruitcake so ancient, it might think it's itself!
With cinnamon sticks, we bake and we bite,
Creating new memories on a cold winter's night.

Socks and shoes by the fire they lie,
Dancing with sparks, as the minutes fly by.
A gingerbread house so wonky and sweet,
With frosting that melts, what a tasty treat!

A cat in a hat, oh what a delight,
Sneaking a nibble from the cookies just right.
As laughter unfolds with each tiny cheer,
Memories brighten through each happy tear!

With every card that we snicker and send,
Wishing joy and fun, spread love without end.
In this magical time, let our spirits be free,
With laughter that's glowing, from you and from me!

Echoes of Joy in Silent Nights

In frosty air, we dance and prance,
With silly hats, we take a chance.
The cat's a reindeer, tail aglow,
As we all laugh and sing, "Ho, ho!"

A snowman's off to buy some snacks,
He tripped and fell, we heard some cracks.
We rolled in snow, what a delight,
Our frozen giggles filled the night.

A squirrel stole a candy cane,
He scurried off, we'd call him vain.
With cocoa spills and marshmallows galore,
We'll laugh till we can't anymore!

In jingle bells, we find the glee,
The dog in costume, what a sight to see!
With memories spun in festive tales,
We'll carry joy beyond the trails.

Radiance Amidst the Falling Snow

Snowflakes fall like confetti bright,
Landing on noses, quite the sight!
A mitten's lost in a snowball fight,
"No, not my face!" is the best invite.

The lights are twinkling, quite askew,
The neighbor's gone rogue with lights of blue.
We'll set up booby traps with glee,
For unsuspecting friends and family!

An icicle's hanging like a frozen sword,
A clever plan, we're never bored.
But down it falls on Uncle Joe,
With laughter, he reigns, our holiday show.

The snowman's dressed in fashion bold,
With sunglasses on, he's fierce, we're told.
In cheerful chaos, we unite,
A festive parade in the frosty light.

Enchanted Moments Beneath the Mistletoe

Under the leaves, we pause to stare,
A mistletoe mishap? We just don't care.
With silly dances, we spin around,
Kisses land where goofballs abound!

A sneaky elf, he tries to peek,
He's named, appropriately, Sneaky Cheek.
"Not on my watch!" I scampered away,
Our goofy antics save the day.

A burly Santa, snorting with zest,
He trips on tinsel, what a fest!
With laughter echoing, we play along,
In the jumbled joy, we all belong.

So grab someone close, and let's take a chance,
With a hearty laugh, we join in the dance.
Beneath the mistletoe, smiles unfold,
In merry moments, warmth is gold.

Candlelit Shadows and Silent Wishes

The candles flicker, casting light,
We're telling ghost stories, oh what a fright!
With shadows dancing on the wall,
"Did you hear that?" we all enthrall!

A wish is made for chocolate cake,
But instead we get a winter quake.
The windows frost with silly dreams,
As we devour marshmallow creams.

The star atop our tree's a kite,
It's swaying low, what a laugh tonight!
With secret wishes and whispered names,
Tangled in laughter, our joy inflames.

As embers glow in the cozy room,
We're sharing cookies to chase the gloom.
In candlelight, where silly thrives,
We'll celebrate joy—forever alive!

Cherished Glimmers in Winter's Hold

Frosty noses twitch and sneeze,
Elves in mittens climb the trees.
Snowmen with hats that don't quite sit,
Dance with joy; their noses split.

Hot cocoa spills, oh what a mess,
Marshmallows bounce, it's pure excess.
Cats in stockings, what a sight,
Prowl for treats in the moonlight.

Reindeer games, it's quite absurd,
Eight of them chase a singing bird.
Jingle bells stuck in a dog's coat,
As he prances, oh what a joke!

Laughter echoes, spirits soar,
In this winter, who could ask for more?
With every chuckle, joy unfolds,
In cherished glimmers, warmth beholds.

Lanterns of Hope in Chill and Snow

Icicles hang like frozen spears,
While penguins strut, full of cheers.
Candles flicker, a dance on the wall,
Making shadows that giggle and crawl.

Socks on the line, a festive sight,
Each one mismatched, adds to the light.
Snowflakes stick to noses, oh dear!
We laugh 'til we cry, spreading cheer.

Fireside tales of socks that roam,
Finding their way back home alone.
Pine trees adorned in colors bizarre,
Spinning ornaments, they raise the bar!

Laughter bubbles, popcorn flies,
As reindeer wear the silliest ties.
Deck the halls with goofy grace,
In every heart, there's a funny place.

Vibrant Echoes from the Hearth

Crackling logs and stories unfold,
As Grandma ups her yarns, bold.
Kittens tumble in the tinsel,
Leaving Christmas cheer in every thimble.

Mittens misplaced, who wore what?
The search is on, oh what a plot!
Hot pie burning on the side,
In this kitchen, joy can't hide.

Cookie dough smeared on every face,
We bake and giggle, a wild race.
Sprinkles flying, it's a sweet storm,
In this laughter, we keep warm.

As carolers croon with kitschy flair,
A cat joins in, unaware of the glare.
Echoes of laughter, bright and clear,
Warm our hearts like eggnog cheer.

Spheres of Light in the Night's Embrace

Glowing bulbs on every street,
Dancing lights with jazzy beats.
Squirrels wrangle with threads of gold,
As the moon laughs, the night unfolds.

Neighbors cheer with cocoa clinks,
Gaggles of geese, oh how they stink!
Wreaths askew on crooked doors,
Their charm amusing, who wants more?

Snowball fights erupt with might,
Snowflakes swirling in playful flight.
As laughter lifts into the night,
We hold these moments, ever bright.

Under stars that twinkle and wink,
We gather 'round and share a drink.
In spheres of light and cozy delight,
Our hearts dance and take flight.

Radiant Hope in Plumes of Snow

In winter's chill, we dance so free,
With socks that clash, oh what a spree!
The snowflakes fall, each one a gem,
As we all slip, like clumsy penguins.

Hot cocoa spills on my brand-new coat,
As Grandma's roast turns into a boat.
We laugh and cheer, like kids on the run,
Wondering if this silly hat's a ton.

Jingle bells clash with a cat's loud yowl,
The Christmas spirit makes us all howl.
With wrapping paper tossed in a heap,
We find lost socks that we had to keep.

So here we are, in a festive whirl,
With cake on our face and a twirl and a swirl.
Amidst all the mess, we cheer and sing,
In the season where laughter is the king.

Morning Glimmers of Awakening Light

The morning light brings joyful cheer,
But so does the smell of burnt roast deer.
Gifts wrapped up with tape gone amiss,
Whose gift is this? Oh, it's the cat's bliss!

With twinkling lights that never stay,
We argue on where the tree should play.
Granddad snores as we sing loud tunes,
Awakening him with jolly tycoons.

Fluffy slippers on our feet so bright,
Socks that don't match? Well, isn't that right?
In the chaos of merry delight,
We make memories that shine so bright.

So raise a toast with duct tape drinks,
Here's to our antics, and all of our jinks!
In this wild season, we laugh and shout,
For what would we do without a little clout?

Cherubs of Joy in a Winter's Dream

Snowflakes tumble in a wild ballet,
While Uncle Joe wears his hat the wrong way.
We sip on cider, as giggles erupt,
At cousin Tim trying to cook up a cup!

We build a snowman with one giant eye,
While the carrot nose makes us all cry.
With mittens mismatched, we run all around,
Finding the treasures that winter has found.

Ornaments falling with every cheer,
As the cat claims them, our greatest fear.
Granny's cookies—oh, what a treat!
That gingerbread man just can't take the heat.

So come one, come all, let's make some cheer,
With laughter and joy, we hug and now steer.
In this silly season, we'll dance and play,
In a winter's dream, we'll find our way.

Melodies of Merriment and Warmth

The carolers come with voices so strong,
But listen closely, they're off-key all along.
With twinkles in eyes and candy canes too,
We laugh at our neighbors, they laugh at us too.

Gifts piled high—will they ever be unwrapped?
Tinsel caught in a cat's purring trap.
We dodge the fruitcake, a weapon of choice,
As Grandpa tells tales with a quiver in voice.

With noses all red and cheeks aglow,
We race down the lane, through powdery snow.
In mittens too big, we try to embrace,
The magic of laughter, it can't be replaced.

So let's celebrate, the joy we impart,
With food fights and fluff that can't tear us apart.
In this season of fun, we cherish the laughter,
For moments like these are what we chase after.

Glowing Reflections of Family Ties

Auntie's fruitcake, oh what a sight,
It glows like a star, but not quite right.
Cousins are giggling, eyes all aglow,
As Uncle Fred fumbles with mistletoe.

Grandma's knitting leaves yarn in a tangle,
While the cat's in the tree, what a jangle!
Laughter erupts as we gather 'round,
In this festive chaos, joy can be found.

Silly hats made of paper and glue,
Who's wearing whose pair? We haven't a clue!
A toast to the moments that spark up delight,
In the warmth of our home, it all feels just right.

Through the fun and the mess, love's shining bright,
These family reflections are pure holiday light.
Such hilarious times weave our stories so fine,
With memories wrapped up, like gifts on a line.

Secrets Hidden in the Hearth's Ember

The fireplace whispers with secrets to tell,
Like Dad's choice of socks, oh can it be well?
Smoky aromas wafting with glee,
As Grandma reveals her wild recipe.

The pine smells of mischief, the lights start to dance,
While we tease little Timmy—he won't take a chance.
Each ornament jingles with paths of mishap,
As we cram in our laughter, oh what a trap!

Rats in the attic or just Auntie's new frock?
What secrets arise when we gather to talk?
With quirks and with giggles, our jokes intertwine,
Wrapped in the warmth that feels utterly divine.

So here's to the secrets, both silly and sweet,
That make our traditions forever repeat.
Savoring each moment, not one to forget,
With love in our hearts and no room for regret.

Festive Wishes on Hoarfrost Wings

Outside it's chilly, but we're all set,
To bake up some cookies, no time for regret!
With sprinkles and icing piled up in a heap,
We'll eat them all fast, not a moment to sleep.

The dog in a scarf, it's a sight to behold,
He's nodding along to the tales we've retold.
Father's bad jokes, oh they make our heads spin,
Yet laughter erupts as we let the fun in.

The carolers sing with a weird little twist,
Their rhythm is off, but our hearts can't resist.
With snowflakes all swirling, like glitter they rise,
We'll catch them in hats and spin stories with ties.

So let's raise a toast to the whimsy in air,
With wishes on wings that twirl everywhere.
Amidst all the giggles and warm colors bright,
It's the spirit of joy that can light up the night.

A Blanket of Gold upon the Earth

The snow settles softly, a gold dusted cheer,
But look who's out shoveling, oh dear, oh dear!
In pjs and boots, they're a comical sight,
Trying to find their way through the night.

Kids throw a snowball, but miss with a splash,
Elder siblings laugh, then make a quick dash.
With sleds in a line, they race down the hill,
While Grandma yells loudly—don't break your will!

Wrapped in too many layers, they tumble and fall,
Each giggle erupts like a sweet, frosty call.
Building snowmen with floppy old hats,
They're waving their arms like the silliest cats!

So here's to the magic that engulfs every soul,
In a world where the laughter can infinitely roll.
A golden blanket, soft whispers and fun,
This holiday season, we're shining like sun!

Luminous Journeys on Winter's Trail

In snowflakes that dance, we twirl with glee,
A snowman's got moves, oh can't you see?
With carrots for noses, they strut with flair,
Chasing each other, without a care.

Idiot squirrels throw snowballs with pride,
Tumbling and rolling, oh what a ride!
Hats worn as shields, they battle the chill,
While children giggle, it's pure winter thrill.

Down hills on our sleds, like rockets we fly,
Face full of snow, but spirits are high!
Hot cocoa in hand, marshmallows afloat,
Warming our hearts, in this wintery coat.

With laughter and joy, this season's a blast,
Remembering moments that go by so fast!
So let's make some memories, snowball by snowball,
For life's little wonders are the best gift of all!

Silvery Echoes of Childhood Glee

Remember those days of mischief and cheer?
With slingshots and snowballs, we conquered each year!
The neighbor's old cat, we stealthily chased,
As he darted away, our laughter replaced.

Crafting our fort with a bucket and pail,
Our snowballs like missiles, we launched without fail!
But one icy hit had us doubled in mirth,
As the dog rolled in snow, oh, what a rebirth!

We'd leave out some cookies, a note and some cheer,
For a jolly old fellow that once a year appears.
With crumbs on the floor and the milk all but gone,
We'd stare at the night, waiting for dawn.

Yet each December brings trouble anew,
With tangled-up lights that just won't undo.
But oh, how we giggle at every small blunder,
As we wrap up our joy in sweet holiday thunder!

Shadows that Sparkle with Delight

Under twinkling lights, a grand tree appears,
Ornaments racing, like skaters on piers.
The cat leaps and pounces, knocking it flat,
While we burst into laughter, "Hey, watch out for that!"

Mega-sized stockings, all stuffed to the brim,
With socks that are filled with surprises within!
Yet, who would have guessed, that one little item,
Is a gift for the dog? Yep, what great timing!

The wrapping paper screams, with Santa's red cheer,
As cats claw and shred it, the mess brings us near!
Wrapping gifts quickly, dodging the wrath,
We giggle and shout, "It's a gift-wrapping path!"

As shadows grow long and laughter takes flight,
We toast to the memories made through the night.
So let's fill our hearts with this whimsy and cheer,
For the spirit of joy is the best gift right here!

Cradles of Laughter and Soft Whispers

Gather 'round kiddies, let's share some fine tales,
Of magical moments and sledding down trails.
When Auntie's wig flew, a sight so absurd,
It landed on Gramps, who just laughed till he burred!

With cookies all doughy, and flour in hair,
We giggled and cackled, oh what a pair!
The dog tried to help; he licked all the dough,
While we shouted with glee, "Hey, you're stealing the show!"

Then came the dance party, with jingle bells sound,
As we pranced around, feet leaving the ground.
Grandma tried moonwalk, her wig flew again,
But we cheered her on, "It's your turn to win!"

In cradles of laughter, our spirits take flight,
We cherish each moment, that sparkles so bright.
For holiday joy, can bring all together,
Sprinkled with laughter, as light as a feather!

Shining Moments Caught in Time

A twinkling bulb swung too low,
The cat jumps up, oh what a show!
Eggnog spills onto the floor,
Grandma's dance? We all want more!

Socks hang later than planned,
All gifts wrapped by the last hand.
A mishap with the ribbon tight,
Unwrap the joy, it's pure delight!

A reindeer nose booms in the night,
Grandpa snorts, what a silly sight!
Mistletoe dips in strange ways,
Each giggle raises the holiday haze!

As snowflakes tap on windows wide,
The kids all run, they wish to glide.
With laughter shared and snacks galore,
These silly moments? We'll ask for more!

Frosty Wings of Cheerful Spirits

A snowman made with two left feet,
Wobbling about, what a funny feat!
With clementines for his grins so bright,
He waves at squirrels with sheer delight!

A snowball fight causes quite a scene,
The dog just ducks, he's so routine.
Kids tumble down, all laughs in the air,
While Mom yells to take care, beware!

Hot cocoa spills, what a silly mistake,
Marshmallows bouncing, oh for goodness' sake!
With whipped cream hats, we toast with cheer,
A frosty day, fun winter gear!

Sticky fingers with candy galore,
Chasing lights but what's behind the door?
With frosty wings and hats askew,
Life's a chuckle with friends, it's true!

An Ode to the Gentle Nightfall

As day drifts softly, shadows play,
The moon peeks out, it's a funny fray!
With twinkling stars that dance so bright,
Even the owls aren't ready for night!

The cookies burned, a crispy treat,
Dogs wear bows and get up on their feet.
Chasing each other, through misty air,
While parents all stop and just stare!

Frost gathers here on vines once green,
As laughter spills like frothy cream.
Each carol sung in offbeat rhyme,
With neighbors joining just in time!

Wrap up the warmth, share tales galore,
Of mishaps and giggles, who could ask for more?
In the gentle hush, let joy abound,
As giggles echo, all around!

Laughter Wrapped in Glittering Tinsel

Glittering tinsel tossed everywhere,
"Oh no!" cries Dad, "What a witty scare!"
The tree's all crooked, but we don't care,
It leans just right, filled with holiday flare!

A cat on the tree? Oh what a shock!
With baubles dangling, a real big block.
When curiosity meets shiny sights,
We simply laugh at the festive fights!

The fruitcake's a joke, an old family tale,
We slice it up, laugh without fail.
With winks and nudges, the stories unfold,
Each year we laugh at the legends retold.

With lights that blink in rhythmic time,
We sing our songs in jumbled rhyme.
Wrapping laughter in ribbons tight,
During this season, we find delight!

Festive Tapestry of Light and Love

Twinkling lights on every tree,
Grandma's fruitcake? Oh, woe is me!
Stockings stuffed, and all in a row,
What's that smell? Uh oh, I don't know!

Sleigh bells ringing, kids full of cheer,
But the dog just ate a gift, oh dear!
Pudding forgotten, it's stuck on the shelf,
Uncle Bob's snoring, we'll take it ourselves!

Wreaths on the door, reindeer on high,
A snowman whose buttons seem to cry.
Snowball fights turning into a mess,
But laughter is what we love, we confess!

So let's raise a glass with a silly toast,
To the times we forget what matters the most!
With hearts aglow and spirits so bright,
We'll dance around in this festive light!

Hope's Embers in the Chill of Night

Frost upon windows, it sparkles like tears,
A cat in a stocking, oh what are the fears?
Hot cocoa spills, but who really minds,
We'll start a new trend with chocolate designs!

Snowflakes fall softly, a view to behold,
But little Timmy's out there acting bold.
His snowsuit is stuffed, he can hardly walk,
He tumbles right down, yet he still wants to talk!

Candles are flickering, the mood's set just right,
But Aunt May's dancing—a curious sight!
With one elbow knock, the tree sways and shakes,
Oops! Now it's a game with the ornaments' breaks!

We gather together, both joyous and loud,
Sharing our laughs, a wonderful crowd.
Under the stars, we whisper our dreams,
In this chilly air, it's laughter that gleams!

Nightingale Serenade of Yuletide

In the kitchen, the chaos reigns supreme,
Flour on faces—the holiday dream!
Cookies misshaped, oh what a delight,
Who knew that baking could cause such a fright?

Carols are sung, off-key and bold,
With a cat in the corner, not quite sold.
Reindeer in pajamas, all covered in fluff,
And a snowman named Fred who can't get enough!

Tinsel is tangled, and gifts overflow,
While Grandpa's wearing an elf hat for show.
Laughter erupts as we pass the pie,
Watch out - that fork flies! Oh my, oh my!

So we gather around with non-stop giggles,
As Uncle Joe tries to show us his wiggles.
With hearts full of joy, we embrace the night,
In this silly moment, everything feels right!

The Shimmer of Love in the Frost

Icicles hanging like crystals of glass,
But Uncle Larry just slipped on some grass!
With laughter and joy, we recall last year,
When snowballs flew—oh dear, oh dear!

Gifts wrapped in paper, a puzzling sight,
Did Aunt Sue mix up the names? What a fright!
The dog's in the corner—he's chewing a shoe,
As we chase him around, giving him his due!

Mittens mismatched, and hats on askew,
But nothing can dim the bright festive hue.
Laughter rings out like bells through the air,
As we dance in the living room, without a care!

So here's to the moments we'll always recall,
The silly, the funny, the ones that enthrall.
With love all around and laughter so true,
We bask in this warmth, and we hope you do too!

Milton Keynes UK
Ingram Content Group UK Ltd.
UKHW021241191124
451300UK00007B/176